BEING
YOUR
BEST!

Your 52 Week Journal Of Self-Discovery

JOI M. STANLEY

Joi M. Stanley
Hillside, New Jersey

Limits of Liability ~ Disclaimer
The author and publisher shall not be liable for your misuse of this material. This book is strictly for informational and educational purposes. The author and publisher do not guarantee that anyone following these techniques, suggestions, tips, ideas, or strategies will become successful. The author and publisher shall have neither liability nor responsibility to anyone concerning any loss or damage caused, or alleged to be caused, directly or indirectly by the information contained in this book.

Cover Design: Panos Lampridis
Editing-Interior Layout: The Self-Publishing Maven
Formatting: Panos Lampridis

ISBN: 978-0-9993860-0-2

Printed in the United States of America

Acknowledgements

My sincere gratitude and thanks to my children, Charles, Naeem, and Jabril, for allowing me to go through the process of releasing the pause on areas of my life that had me stuck. As a mother, it's not always easy to admit that you're flawed. The work that I went through to begin the journey of 'Being My Best' was not an easy one. It has had me very uncomfortable; a process that I had to go through on my path to becoming the 'best mother' I could be to you.

Thanks to my mother, Sandy, for always believing in me, and knowing that at the end of the day, I will do what is best. To my father El-Sid, thank you for being in my life and allowing me to love you in ways I never imagined possible. To my brothers and sisters, thank you for your patience, for your love and allowing me to just be "ME". Although I may not see you nearly as much as I would like, know that I hold a special place in my heart for each of you.

*A very special THANKS to my husband, Ray, for not always understanding, BUT putting up with my flaws while I went through each phase of the table of contents in this journal, and discovered things about myself that made me (us) very uncomfortable. You have been there for me through all of my ups and down's and always have been by my side **no matter what**! I would not have been able to go through this process of self-discovery without you! Thank you for loving me unconditionally!*

Thank You, Gleshia Joyner Givens for answering the call to join the 'Being Your Best' movement. Thank You, Dixie Lincoln Nichols, for holding me accountable week after week for the past year to get this journal completed. Thanks to the "Women In My Circle" (you know who you are) who know that I'm not perfect, but have faith enough in me to correct my mistakes.

This self-discovery process would not have even been a thought without my business mentor Mrs. Lucinda Cross-Otiti! Without you seeing in me what I didn't see in myself and holding me to task, the birth of this journal would be late delivery. I truly thank GOD for allowing you to pour into me along this journey.

And last, but most certainly not least, to my other mother, Dorothy Protzman, THANK YOU for sharing all the many emails of almost every single title of this 52-week journal. You planted this seed over a year ago by sending me my work posted on my social media pages. You said that I needed to put them in book form, well, here it is, and I thank you from the bottom of my heart for always being supportive of me and loving me.

Dedicated

To:
My grandchildren, Amani, Aliyah, and Jaxon, I pray that you grow to become strong, courageous, and empowering adults that aren't afraid to stand up for your beliefs.
*I pray that when you're old enough, you will understand that your mental and spiritual well-being is the most important area of your life that must be nurtured and maintained with balance. Never allow anyone to compromise your soul and **live abundantly**. Strive to keep your integrity and remember that your word is your bond.*
I promise to leave a legacy in which you will be proud to call me GiGi.

To:
My sister/cousin, Sharon, you showed me the importance of living life every day to the fullest and to not take the simple things for granted. Seeing you stay strong and always encouraging me when you were experiencing a major health crisis, and never, ever, had a woe is me attitude, showed me what 'Being Your Best' is all about. You taught me the meaning of staying true to who you are despite the odds stacked against you.
YOU NEVER GAVE UP! You are MY living proof that you ARE the language which you speak to yourself. You spoke life into your existence every day, and are blessed to receive a second chance to LIVE YOUR BEST LIFE! Thank you for believing in me and understanding how important the Being Your Best mission is to me.

With all my love,

Joi

Introduction

I created this journal because my goal is to help as many people as I can to become their best possible self. I envision a world in which everyone can be happy with who they are, love themselves unconditionally, and be unapologetic about it! Many of us struggle to live in a society that can be so unforgiving. I hope that through the process of releasing the pause on what has kept you from being your best, your world will open up to abundant possibilities. But this process can only be successful if you are willing to do the work.

Once upon a time, I was taught that it was selfish to think about myself before caring for others, I've learned to the contrary, that if I don't do the work of working on me, I am no good for anyone.

I pray that you find the journey to self-discovery uncomfortable. I know that sentence sounds weird. However, if you do, I will know that I did my job in capturing some of the key area's in your life that need to be addressed and ultimately put you on the road to Being Your Best!

Are you ready? Let's begin!

The questions in this book are designed to establish clarity and open up new possibilities for you as you begin the work of re-discovering yourself.

Do Not Rush this process!

Read *each* question *daily* (For 7 Days) then journal your results. This process is designed for you to look at each question and possibly identify what may be new to you from day to day and its manifestation. Speeding through this journal of self-discovery and not fully do the work, will only rob you of your full experience. Be patient with what you uncover (or not). What may seem like nothing to you now will have a way of showing up for you later.

Your List to Self-Discovery

1. Becoming Your Best
2. What Role Do You Play?
3. Does The Opinion Of Others Matter?
4. How well do you know those in your circle?
5. Are your Scales Balanced?
6. Becoming Uncomfortable
7. How BIG are you playing?
8. Are you playing too comfortable?
9. Pause Language
10. Beware of your "self" stories
11. The Power of Choice.
12. The Power Positivity Pledge
13. Your belief of your "Fears" can be greater than your belief in "You"
14. Become Fearless in your life
15. Take Action
16. Celebrate becoming Fearless
17. Control how things shows up in your life
18. Understanding and Manifesting Positive ENERGY
19. Being in the "Now" the process of how you see yourself
20. You are in control of your destiny, so say "Yes" to new possibilities.
21. Accepting Unacceptable Behavior
22. Are you a dumping ground for bad behavior?
23. Unacceptable behavior can destroy your soul.
24. Regaining Power of Unacceptable Behavior
25. The power of your "NO"
26. Setting Boundaries

Week 1

"The best project you will ever work on is you."

Becoming Your Best!

We are what we repeatedly do. Excellence, then, is not an act, but a habit. – Aristotle

Once you begin the work to become your best, there are certain disciplines and new habits of thinking that will start to support your progress. You will need to consider how you will integrate these habits into your way of being as you begin this journey. It's not enough to have the idea of wanting the best in life; you must commit to how you will make the necessary changes to become who you are meant to be. It takes determination, discipline, and a lot of practice to implement change over time. Embark on this journey of self –discovery by:

1. Exploring who you are beyond all measures and become uncomfortable enough to begin to understand the power that you have to manifest to the fullest potential of self.

2. Taking this journey and fall madly in love with you.

3. Embracing your life's unique set of circumstance because you are uniquely different.

4. Learning how to heal yourself through healing and forgiveness.

5. Telling your inner critic where to go.

6. Learning to step into your self-importance, because you matter.

7. Understanding how your soul speaks to you through intuitiveness.

8. Learning to quiet your mind and relax through the process of self-care.

9. Learning to take care of your body, and create a life that you adore.

10. Making the difference that only you can make.

The next 52 weeks will explore all of the above topics and then some. 'Being Your Best,' through the process of self-care, self-discovery, and allowing you the chance to release the pause on what has kept you stuck is the journey will you take starting now.

Over the next week, select a specific but different topic each day and journal your thoughts on how they pertain to your self-discovery process. Allow yourself to become vulnerable. Allow yourself to see who you truly are. Learn to be transparent and see your way through the process. Welcome to the self-discovery process of becoming your best. Celebrate the choice to take this time to invest in no one else but you.

Week 2

*"How others see you is not important,
how you see yourself
means everything."*

What Role Do You Play?

It is important you understand the 'allowed' role you play in the lives of others. This week, pay attention to the perception that others have of YOU, see if it aligns with your actions. Remember, Perception is "Everything" to some and "Relative" to others. Here are some questions to consider for this week.

- Are you always willing to play along even when you don't want to?

....

- Do you find yourself becoming easily annoyed at certain personality types, i.e., wieners, loud talk, hand gestures, etc.?

....

- Do you sit back in the cut and just add to the scenery?

....

- Are you the life of the party? And everyone will know who you are before the night ends?

....

Be clear about who you are to *yourself.* 'Being Your Best' means knowing who you are, so others cannot label you to be someone/something that you're not. Journal your discovery of what you feel as to your perception to others.

....
....
....
....
....
....
....
....
....

Week 3

"Your opinion of me is none of my business."

Other People's Opinion

How important is it for you to be liked by others? Does this play a critical part in keeping the stress out of your interactions with others? Are you playing the role of a peacemaker and paying less attention to how you feel? Are you compromising your true feelings to have a favorable opinion from whom you associate? Here are some additional questions to consider on this week.

- Do you become stressed over relationships where you're uncertain if you are liked by someone or a group of people? If so, why?

....

- Do you find yourself always agreeing so that others don't think negatively of you? If so, why?

....

Subconsciously, our minds will move us to act according to what our surroundings tell us. Now that those questions have been asked and answered, do their opinions matter? If so, why? In this week of discovery, write out your thoughts and the solution to stop basing your life on other people's opinion.

....
....
....
....
....
....
....
....
....
....
....
....
....

Week 4

"Protect your circle; invest in people who will feed you as much good as you feed them."

How well do you know those in your circle?

Take this week to analyze the people you associate with, friends, family, etc. Here are some questions to consider this week.

- Do they leave a positive impact on you?

....

- Can you identify those that you feel you have to put more work into keeping the relationship?

....

- Do the people in your circle value you?

....

This process is not going to be an easy one. Often once the adjustments' made, you start to see things from a new point of discovery. Change is good. It means that you are paying attention to you! Journal your thoughts and embrace whatever is about to happen. **Welcome to the Self Discovery Process Of Being Your Best!**

What do you need to do about your circle? Journal your thoughts this week.

....
....
....
....
....
....
....
....
....
....
....
....

Week 5

"Every next level of your life will bring next level friends who will change the look of who is sitting at your table."

Are your scales balanced?

Do you have more Doers, or do you have more Naysayers in your circle? This week, decide who is on your team. *Who can help you get to the next level?*

- Who has made a difference in your life?

....

- Who has been your opposition?

....

This won't be an easy assessment but a necessary one to know with whom you should move forward. Who do you need to embrace more or pull back from? Reflect on that this week and journal your discoveries.

....
....
....
....
....
....
....
....
....
....
....
....
....
....
....
....
....
....

Week 6

"Success of anything begins with becoming uncomfortable. That's when you know that you must be doing something right,"

Becoming Your Best Will Make You Uncomfortable

If you're not uncomfortable at the table, then you are not at the right table. Successful people tend to surround themselves with the same type of individuals and conversations that lead you to want to know more or become engaged in the possibility of ventures created between the two of you. Some questions to consider.

- Ask yourself who is seated at your table that ideas can flow back and forth within the conversation?

....

- Who can push you to Be Your Best?

....

- Who can you help get to the next level?

....

You must be able to give in order to receive. This journey through your discovery process should make you uncomfortable. If it does, then you are truly doing the work to become your best. Think of one place or thing that makes you uncomfortable and tackle it this week. Make sure you journal the results.

....
....
....
....
....
....
....
....
....
....
....
....

Week 7

"Permit yourself to live a big life. Step into the greatness of who you are meant to be. Stop playing small and show the world how great you are by playing big."

How BIG are you playing?

Are you surrounding yourself with people who are playing big? How BIG are they playing? Pick them apart one by one and analyze their movement. Aside from you, who are their friends? Here are a few more questions to consider.

- What contributions are you making to those who sit at your table? What is your give back?

....

- Are you making yourself available to learn from them or busy being a know it all?

....

- Are you asking the right questions to help you get to the next level?

....

Playing BIG can be a great thing when you surround yourself with the right people. However, playing BIG requires giving back BIG. Take your time this week and think about how big you want to play. Write your plans and thoughts on how to move forward.

....
....
....
....
....
....
....
....
....
....
....

Week 8

"Every new level of your life will require a different version of you."

Are you playing too comfortable?

What are you doing? Are you putting yourself in the company of those who will elevate you and hold you accountable for what you say you want to accomplish? Are or will you do the same in return? Or, are you comfortable in being in the place in which you sit, not being satisfied? The level up process will make you re-evaluate how you are living, make you uncomfortable and will require change.

- Are you ready to get uncomfortable?

....

- What do you think you may have to do differently to become uncomfortable?

....

Journal ways in which becoming uncomfortable will create positive change for you this week. List what new possibilities can come from your becoming uncomfortable.

....
....
....
....
....
....
....
....
....
....
....
....
....
....
....
....

Week 9

"What you tell yourself, you become."

PAUSE Language

Pay attention to your language this week, how you speak to yourself, as well as, to others. Is it positive language or language that will bring negative results? Are you using words like, try, can't, maybe, or perhaps? These are words that can alter the direction of what you want.

- Don't give surface answers. Dig deep to be able to access yourself honestly.

Example:
- Are you using too much profanity to get your points across?

....

- Are you judging yourself harshly or not seeing yourself in a positive way?

....

- Are you allowing others to speak to you any way they choose to? Especially if the end results of the conversation leaves you feeling worse than before the conversation even started.

....

Raise your personal and reflective radar this week. Be open enough with yourself to see clearly how your language with self and others can affect everything you do. Words are POWERFUL, be extra careful with how you use them on YOU. Write down what you discover.

....
....
....
....
....
....
....
....

Week 10

*"Make sure your worst enemy is not
living between your two ears.
Change your story, change your life."*

Beware of your 'self' stories

Examine your belief system this week. What belief system have you been holding on to that's keeping you from releasing the pause button on your dreams. Are you allowing these beliefs to hold you hostage? Are the stories that you have been holding on to keeping you from your greatness?

We all have stories that we have told ourselves, but how we deal with them can be life changing. Are you allowing your stories to keep you from getting to the next level in life? Our stories can become our safety net like a baby who holds on to their security blanket. These stories, if allowed, can keep you stuck and comfortable.

- List 3 stories that you have told yourself you've been holding on to that is keeping you from leveling up.

- ....
- ....
- ....

- If you were to release the pause button on these stories, what would your life look like?

....

- Go as far as rewriting your story. Write your new story with the outcome the way you would like to be.

....
....
....

Look at them carefully, allow yourself to feel the new story. See yourself in the new story. Become the Star in the "New" story that will take you to the next level. Here is more space for you to begin again.

....
....
....
....

50

Week 11

"Everything in your life is a reflection of a choice you've made. If you want a different result make a different choice,"

The Power Of Choice

Choose to speak nothing but positivity this week. No matter how difficult you may find it to be. Do not allow anyone to take you out of your good path and saturate your thoughts with positivity. Choose to let nothing else fill up your space.

- List one thing you can do each day this week to remain positive.

....

....

- List one thing you may have to change/remove from your daily routine to receive the positive energy that you seek this week.

....

....

Chart your progress by journaling what happened during your important choice for this week.

....

....

....

....

....

....

....

....

....

....

....

....

....

....

Week 12

"Take the Pledge"

The power of positivity pledge

I will no longer allow negative thought or feelings to drain me of my energy. Instead, I shall focus on all the good that is in my life. I will think it, feel it, speak it, and by doing so, I will send out vibes of positive energy into the world and be grateful for all the wonderful things it will attract into my life. By doing all of these things, I know that I am on the road to becoming my best.

Starting this week, we're adding something to mix it up a bit. For the next 21 days, (Yes, this is in addition to the work in the book) practice the agenda from last week. *The Power of Positive Thinking* let the <u>process of positivity</u> become a new way of life for you. Release the pause on the old language you used to speak.   Practice the Art of Positive Thinking and Speak Language that will bring forth positive results. Remember you be-come what you think. Write a positive sentence each day below. Happy journaling!

- _____
  _____
- _____
  _____
- _____
  _____
- _____
  _____
- _____
  _____
- _____
  _____
- _____
  _____
- _____
  _____
- _____

- _____
- _____
- _____
- _____
- _____
- _____
- _____
- _____
- _____
- _____
- _____
- _____

"The 21 day
power of positivity challenge"

(Refer back to this page for 21 days...... DO YOUR WORK!)

Week 13

*"Don't let the fear of what could happen
be the reason
you make nothing happen,"*

Your belief in your Fears can be greater than your belief in "You."

The definition of fear is false evidence appearing real. In other words, allowing yourself to get all worked up over something without being sure of the outcome. Being fearless doesn't mean eliminating fear, it means knowing how to leverage fear. Although reported to be a healthy emotion, part of fear is instinct. Some fears are learned, most are taught and dictate the actions you take. It takes a willing participant to allow fear to take over.

Take this week to identify what 'Fears' you've held hostage. We all have fears, even conquered ones.

- Write them down so that you can clearly identify this fear.

....
....

- Stare the fear directly in the face. Write out why you have these fears, and what they're keeping you from obtaining.

....
....

Journal how this exercise makes you feel, and what emotions are starting to surface. Become bigger than the Fears. Tap into the power that you have over them. Write out the concise details of how you will conquer your fears. You've Got This!

....
....
....
....
....
....
....
....
....
....
....
....

Week 14

"When you honestly don't care what any-one thinks about you, you have reached a dangerously high level of fearlessness."

Become Fearless in Your Life

How are you letting fear of what others are saying or what you think they will say about you, affect your ability to become FEARLESS. Examine the different types of relationships that you have from family to your close friends. What fear are you holding on to regarding your relationships?

- Who are you allowing to hold you hostage because they may know something about you that can be damaging to your reputation? Allowing them to own your power.

....

- Who are you fearful of because they play BIGGER than you And allowing the spirit of envy to take control?

....

- In what areas of your life are you letting your fear of accomplishment hold you back because you don't want to be ridiculed by your family or friends.

....

- Create an additional list of other fears that may be holding you back from being Fearless. Let all the secrets out so that you can begin to own your power.

Be transparent in your journaling this week. Only you hold the key to releasing what is keeping you from becoming 'fearless' in every aspect of your life. What an incredible journey, don't allow fear to stop you from living your best life. Have a fantastic time journaling this week. You're getting closer to Being Your Best.

....
....
....
....
....
....

Week 15

"The difference between who you are and who you want to be is what you do. Doing takes action."

Take Action

Identify action steps that can help you to rid yourself of the fears you've listed. Then put a plan of action in effect. Do not just write down the things you need to do and then do nothing, get uncomfortable while doing this work. Journal your feelings while doing this exercise. Be as transparent as possible and allow yourself to be open to seeing who you are.

- What does Fear look like to you? The only way to become fearless is to understand what fear looks like to you.

....

- What is one fear that you struggle with that you would like to rid yourself of?

....

- How do you see this fear showing up in your life? And what ways do you need assistance releasing this fear?

What is your ultimate plan to take action?

....
....
....
....
....
....
....
....
....
....
....
....
....
....
....
....

Week 16

"Once you become fearless,
you become limitless."

Celebrate becoming FEARLESS

By now, if you have been doing the work on discovering who you are regarding 'fear.'

- What progress have you seen over the last few weeks?

....

- Have you come far enough to celebrate your wins over the discovery of your fears?

....

- What have your fears represented in your life?

....

Take this week to review your past work. It's never too late to start over, which is, the best part about transparency. Here's to the beginning of the New You! Celebrate anyway for all of the work you have done thus far.

....
....
....
....
....
....
....
....
....
....
....
....
....

Week 17

"No one has power over you unless you give it to them. You are in control of your life, and your choices control how things show up in your life."

Control how things show up in your life

Amazingly, in all my research regarding this topic, there were a few issues that seem to be most prevalent in them all. Controlling people exhibit certain traits that are characteristic of the control behavior. This week, ask yourself if any of these questions point to you, or if you have close relationships with them. Either way, it will give you something to think about if you are serious about being on the road to Being Your Best. What are the traits? See below and journal about one each day to see if it is showing up in your life. Here are some questions to ponder.

- Do you have any relationships that make you feel stressed, so to keep the peace you give in?

....

- Are you judgmental or over critical of others?

....

- Do you have a problem admitting when you are wrong and always want to be right?

....

- Do you always need to have the last word?

....

- Do you have trouble keeping a meaningful relationship or do you easily let people walk out of your life?

....

Keep in mind that those who want to be in control are not trying to hurt you, they're trying to protect themselves. Remind yourself that the behavior exhibited isn't personal. If you like to be in control or know someone who does, manipulation is also a trait to be aware of. Keep it real with yourself this week. Enjoy the journey.

....
....
....

Week 18

"Positive energy can heal the universe,"

Understanding and Manifesting Positive ENERGY

There's a saying "things happen the way they're meant to happen." But how so? Through the unification of our many selves, the ongoing practice of being present within your own body and being present regarding your daily experiences, your energy will begin to align. You will automatically start to strengthen your aura, your mind, and your willpower when you possess good energy. Then you will begin the process of conscious manifestation.

No matter the methods you find and learn, the bottom line is that in order to manifest, you have to know what you want and why, and perhaps most importantly, what will happen once you get what you want. To get those answers, you need to begin to know yourself more completely. This week as yourself these questions:

- Why do I do the things that I do on a daily basis?

....

- Why do I think the way I do? (my thoughts, my perception, my feelings)

....

- Are these my true feelings, or was this how I was taught to feel?

....

- What am I really afraid of?

....

If your answers don't come right away, don't try to force it. Just continue observing, asking and feeling. Eventually, this will open you up for answers, invite energy for change and begin to set the intention of permission to get your information, on "Who" you're becoming.

Use this week to pay close attention to your energy and how you do things. See if your results are from the energy you put out. If not, journal how you deal what you get from this exercise. Get to know you. Don't cheat yourself! Do the work.

Week 19

"Being present is the only moment that matters."

Being in the "NOW" the process of how you see yourself

How do you react to things that don't go the way you want them to go? Are you multi-tasking, instead of being in the moment of each experience? Are you truly aware of who you are and the actions you take in situations as a whole?

Falling into the awareness of who you are reveals your feelings and how you react to things. The more awareness you have participating in that experience, the more control, focus clarity and enjoyment you're able to create and receive. I only have one thing for you to ask yourself every day. When I am working am I in the "NOW"? Do this:

- Look back at the opening of this week's journal. How did you react when things didn't go your way?

....

- Were you multitasking instead of being in the moment?

....

- Were you aware of who you are and the actions taken in situations as a whole?

....

How many times have had to shift and do something different? Did you just go along with the change or did you do something to redirect the outcome? Be sure to stay in your moments by paying close to attention your actions and journaling this week. You should be starting to feel a shift. Are you getting uncomfortable yet?

....
....
....
....
....
....
....
....
....
....

Week 20

"Your blessings can only be blocked if you allow them to be!"

You are in control of your destiny, so say "YES" to new possibilities

Allow yourself to be open to change for change is good! Think of all the great possibilities you can have on this journey towards 'Being Your Best' if you just say "YES" to what feels good to your soul. I used to block my blessing by always, always, always, second guessing myself. I would think to do something, and my energy would be all in, and then before you know it, I let the doubt/fear set in, comfortably. I finally learned that I was in control of my destiny, and every time I altered the path set before me the first time, I was surrendering to the fear of my greatness.

- Take a minute to reflect this week's time when you didn't say "YES" to something that you wished you had because the doubt/fear set in.

....
....

To manifest, you preferably want to get all your spiritual, mental, emotional and physical energy in one place, merged, moving in one direction, like a river, carrying you in the direction of 'Being Your Best.' Your goals don't have to be linear, a river curves and bends, but it does have to flow forward to progress. Your blessings will manifest themselves if you allow the natural path to direct its course.

- Imagine what the possibilities would have been and you took control of your destiny and said "YES" Imagine what change of life could be possible if you were to take MORE control.

....
....

Let go and let life happen. Your blessings are blocked if YOU allow them to be! What do you need to open yourself to and how will you work better at not blocking your blessings?

....
....
....

Week 21

"You may not be able to control someone's negative behavior, but you can control how long you participate in it."

Accepting unacceptable behavior

How often do you walk away from situations angry with yourself for not handling things differently? Getting to know yourself starts with the conscious decision to pay attention to your thoughts and behaviors, more importantly, what you allow and accept.

'Being Your Best' requires discipline, which is the key to building the will power to accept or decline what is good for your energy. This discipline will also manifest the actions that you carry out with more power to activate your true identity and self.

The type of behavior you allow around you speaks to your character and willingness to change. This week, examine how you interact and connect with people.

- Are you allowing yourself to give a free pass to those who are displaying unacceptable behavior?

....

Look carefully and excuse no one; this is critical to you being able to release that pause button on how you allow others to behave around you.

....
....
....
....
....
....
....
....
....
....
....
....
....

Week 22

"People will notice the change in your attitude toward them but won't see their behavior that made you change."

Are you a dumping ground for bad behavior?

When you accept behavior that doesn't benefit you, you become a battlefield for others to dump on. How many relationships do you have that make you question the validity when you're not in their company? If you spend any time examining the relationships you have, start there. How many battlefield situations have you found yourself involved in and how were you able to walk away from with no wounds?

Sometimes it's helpful to ask yourself a few assessment questions, which may look like the following:

- Were my expectations not realized and therefore left me angry, mad or disappointed by the person's behavior?

....

....

- Have I been down this road with this person before and therefore I shouldn't expect any other type of behavior?

....

....

No matter your answer, keep in mind that once you allow someone to dump their problems, anger or aggression on you, you bear the weight of their misery. You now have given them power over you to control your next movements. Transference of energy is a REAL THING. We have all experienced it a time or two in our lives but understand there are some who will always stay stuck in that place because they have pressed the pause button on themselves from being happy. Pay very close attention to the dumping process. Regaining control may require you to take a break from unacceptable behaviors of others. Know that it's okay to maintain your mental health. Take some time this week to see if you're allowing anyone to dump on you. Be clear as to how to recognize them. List them so that you are clear about who they are. Identify how you will regain your power from them. List how you will make that happen next to their names. When you can see it clearly in black and white, there is an energy that will come over you. Being CLEAR of what change you need to make to Becoming Your Best.

Week 23

*"Bad Behavior **can** and **will** destroy relationships, but more importantly **accepting unacceptable behavior** for an extended period can destroy your soul."*

Unacceptable behavior can destroy your soul

It can make you have self-doubt and feel worthless. Read this sentence out loud again. Reflect on it for a while, then ask yourself if you've been honest with yourself over the past two weeks. Reflect on the type of relationship you have with this person. Ask yourself if:

- They are worthy to be in your life at all.

....

....

- The relationship can be salvaged.

....

....

Take a look at the list you created from last week. If your answer is yes, then let's start working on ways to better interact with them. It will take some time to go over the list again. This time, carefully look at your remarks from last week and notice at this moment how you feel about the type of behavior you've have allowed from them. Embrace the feeling as you now get to create a new possibility for change in the relationship you have with them. List the change and embrace it as well. Feel that change as if it has already taken place. You have just begun the process of the new possibility of this person, and they don't even know it. You now *own your power.* Celebrate your progress. It's time to heal. In your journaling this week, take steps toward feeling better about the NEW YOU! Which is vital to restoring your soul!

....

....

....

....

....

....

....

Week 24

*"Sometimes your decision to forgive
is simple when you're not ready to
kick them out of your life,"*

Regaining Power of Unacceptable Behavior

Stop accepting bad behavior! Sounds simple right? But you know from the work you've done over the past three weeks that it's not as simple as it sounds. If the relationship is worth saving, now the work must begin. Others will see that you will no longer allow them to change the flow of your energy. Once again, take a look at your list you created.

- Release the pause button on what has held you back from taking your power back.

....
....

- Take action this week to determine who stays in YOUR LIFE.

....
....

- Then set a plan of action of how you will have that much-needed conversation.

....
....

Imagine the possibility of what the conversation will look like and journal your thoughts on this and your outcome this week.

....
....
....
....
....
....
....
....
....
....
....

Week 25

"Just say "NO" if it no longer serves you"

The power of your "NO"

Knowing when to say no is one of the most powerful tools of your life's existence. Saying no helps in keeping in integrity with prioritization, it gives you a sense of control of who you are, it gives you power, and tells people that your time is valuable and you know it. Saying "NO" is hard, as we want to please others. We want to look like we're capable of doing everything. The good news is there are a lot of nuances even though it's on two letters. When faced with an "ask," that is outside of your yes orbit, you have six ways to choose your "NO." Depending on the situation decide which choice "NO" is right for you.

Delegate: "NO, it's not for me, but here's the person I will assign it to." Here you have delegated the task to someone who you feel can get the job done. Freeing up your time.

Deflect: "NO, isn't for me, but I can connect you with someone who can do this for you." Referring them to someone else.

Delay: "NO, I can't do it right now, but if I get an opportunity to, I will let you know. Taking the burden off of you as it's something that you don't want to do anyway.

Decline: "NO, this is a direct no." No, I can't, or I won't do it. No reason necessary.

Discard: "NO, This may be the hardest of all as it can feel rude. But is a necessary tactic in this information age. The "ask," that may come via text or email. Some feel that it is a simpler way to get someone to commit based on convenience. However, it is a lesser way of communication and can seem impersonal to respond with a "sorry in advance, NO."

No matter which way you choose to exercise your power of "NO" the best feeling in the world is to say "NO" and feel good about it. This week, make a "NO" list. It's all about you and your *'Power to Control'* the things that mean you no good. Here is the one area where you actually get to be in control. Say "NO" to the things that do not make you feel good. If it isn't helping you in your journey towards 'Being Your Best,' then *just say no!* Each day this week journal your discovery of how you used your power of NO.

Week 26

*"You teach people how to treat you,
standing firm in your power of "NO"
draws a line in the sand."*

Setting Boundaries

In my research, I've learned that the use of the word "NO" has two faces. The one we turn toward ourselves, and the one that creates boundaries between yourself and others. The struggle to strengthen our internal no is the one we address to our self-destructive impulses and the struggle with which we are most familiar. "No" controls our events of road rage, and also the urge for that drink or cigarette. Also called "No" self-discipline! Examine how you are using your "No." Just say no this week to anything that you don't want to do, "And Make No Apology!" You get to exercise the power of being ok with decisions you make. Be open and honest with yourself this week while exercising your "NO." Make sure you're using it to best benefit you. Feel your power this week.

- List daily where you feel your "NO" is showing up for you.

....

....

- Make mental notes as to where you should have inserted your use of "NO."

....

....

Feel your power as you journal your progress.

....

....

....

....

....

....

....

....

....

....

....

Week 27

"You have to learn to say NO without feeling guilty; Setting boundaries is healthy, You need to learn to respect and take care of yourself."

No, the Shield of Exploitation

Without feeling guilty, by now, you should feel 'Powerful' in your ability to say "No." It's about 'You, ' and you shouldn't feel guilty for using it. Understand that your time is valuable and should be used to best benefit you. No, is a moment of clear choice. It announces, however indirectly, something affirmative about you. For example: "I will not sign" – because it is not my truth. "I will not join your committee, help with your kids, review your project" – because I am committed to some important project of my own. My personal favorite: "Count me out" – because I'm not comfortable, not in agreement, not on your bandwagon. "No, thank you," because you might feel hurt if I turn down your invitation, my needs take priority. The "NO" is an affirmation of self and implicitly acknowledges personal responsibility; It says that while each of us interacts with others, and loves, respects, and values those relationships, we do not and cannot allow ourselves always to be influenced by them. The strength we draw from saying "No" is that it underscores this hard truth of maturity and shields you from exploitation. Ask yourself:

- Do you value your use of "NO."

....
....

- Do you recognize its power if you use it correctly?

....
....

Journal if you agree or not, but give justification with an example if you do not. You will need to look back over the course of the months to see if your self-discovery journey has you looking at your belief system on your use of the word "No."

....
....
....
....

Week 28

"Find your voice and show the world that you have the power and the choice to use your "NO"!

Find Your Voice

Just say 'No' because you can! Pay attention this week to whether or not you're saying 'No.' Pay attention to your stress levels for accepting things where you should've said 'No.' It will take some time to get used to this process of liberation. Don't be surprised if others start to become angry at your decision to use your power. Remember, saying no to someone means you are no longer serving them, but serving "You." This week of journaling should feel perfect.

- Write a time when you said 'Yes' to someone that you should have said 'No' to. Explore the space this decision had you in.

....

....

- Begin creating new possibilities. Describe ways not to allow yourself to be in this place again.

....

....

Take time this week getting to know this new 'You' who has no problem with using your different ways to say "No."

....
....
....
....
....
....
....
....
....
....
....
....

Week 29

"Self-care isn't selfish, it's necessary."

Understanding Self-Care

One of the most important topics of 'Being Your Best' is 'Self-Care' provided for you, by you. 'Self Care' is about identifying your own needs and taking the necessary steps to meet them. It is the act of nurturing self and taking the proper care of 'you.' And treating yourself just as good or **better** than you treat others. Example: when traveling by plane, the first thing the flight assistant says, in the event of an emergency, you are to put on your oxygen mask first before you assist others. We can only be good for anyone else if we care for ourselves first. How easy is it for us to forget. So that you can see how important this is for your survival, take this week to list all the ways that you care and do for others. Each day I want you to journal what you have done for someone else. Do not neglect the smallest of thing. i.e., making a copy for someone at work, or picking up something from the store at lunchtime for a co-worker. These small things play a large part in identifying your role as a care giver to others.

- Journal daily, what you have done for someone else.

....

- How much time did it take away from you?

....

- Did the act of caring for someone else' need interfere with your own plans?

....

Be open with this exercise so that you may gauge the amount of time you're truly catering to others. It is important to see where your spending your time.

....
....
....
....
....
....

Week 30

"You are no good for anyone else if you don't care for yourself first"

Why is Self-Care Important?

How much time did you assess spending on others? The act of caring for someone else can begin to consume your life if you allow it. You can spend so much of your time as I call it "rescuing other people" until you find yourself worn out and stressed over caring for someone else, which can easily turn into neglect for self. You will become empty, not allowing time for yourself to refuel. Balancing stress and the activity of our daily lives brings a sense of peace and well-being to our minds, body, and soul. When we continue to ignore our own needs, we can quickly become unhappy with the choices we make, life and most importantly, self. Many began to suffer from low self-esteem, and start to feel resentment towards others. Why is self-care so important? It brings that balance into existence to make your life happy and whole again. It reaffirms the importance of treating yourself as a worthwhile person and showing that you're valuable, competent and deserving. What are you doing to recharge?

- Have you been neglecting your self-care?

....
....

- What excuses, if any have you told yourself that have kept you from caring for self?

....
....

- How important is self-care to you?

....
....

- Create your self-care list. The ways you have spent time caring for you.

....
....

Once you have completed this exercise, each day this week, come up with two additional ways you can introduce self-care into your weekly routine. Don't think small. Be kind to yourself. Put into the universe ways of taking care of YOU as if you were planning the ultimate self-care week for someone else. Treat yourself as good, as you have been treating everyone else.

Week 31

"It's not selfish to have the "me first" attitude when it comes to your self-care."

Strategies for Self-Care

Although I make self-care a part of my daily routine, and highly encourage you to do the same, it's essential for a healthy lifestyle. Making time for your self-care is one thing, but are you allowing others and other things to interrupt the time you have set aside for self. Never feel bad to tell someone that you are busy taking care of "Self." Though not easy for some, it will take time and practice to understand the importance of taking care of you. Even those of us (Me) who think we have this self-care thing down pat have often allowed other things to interrupt our self-care routine.

One of the **first** things I recall doing was setting a goal for myself of how many times per month I wanted to do something for me. It started out as once a month because I thought it would be expensive, ha, ha, ha. I laugh because I spent so much money doing for someone else and had to justify spending money on me. Crazy Right? The **next** thing that I did for myself was put it on my calendar as a date with myself. And let me be clear, self-care is about you! It's not about inviting your friends to go to that spa with you. Although that can add to the fun of the day, this day is about you enjoying you. **It's about** getting to know you and caring for no one else during this time. Most importantly, self-care is something that you must **actively plan** rather than something that just happens. So now that you know what self-care is, and what you have been doing for others:

- Look at your calendar and schedule your first (next) self-care experience.

....

- How much time do you think is appropriate for you to spend on yourself?

....

- During each self-care experience, identify an area that you want to work on growing toward Being Your Best.

....

Take time to doing this exercise and take care of yourself. Take the opportunity to spoil yourself and go all out on you. Enjoy this process as it's all about YOU!

Week 32

"Self-care is not Selfish!"

What SELF-CARE is not

It's crucial to know what self-care is not. It shouldn't be something we force ourselves to do or something that you don't enjoy doing. Self-care is something that should refuel you and not **"A Selfish Act."** It's not something we force ourselves to do or to ponder whether we need it. Self-care is something necessary to take care of ourselves so we will have the strength to take care of others.

Remember when I said earlier in another week of exercises that, I'm not good for anyone else if I don't care for me? Ultimately, as crazy as it may sound, self-care isn't just about you. Applying the basic principles surrounding self-care, the one principle which stands in the forefront is Balance.

Balance is key in identifying the many roles that play a big part of our lives involving self-care. Putting others before you only gives them a part of the whole you. There is a necessary balance that should be implemented to continue living a happy and healthy lifestyle. This week, pay attention to you! Daily, write yourself a letter stating your self-care intentions. In this letter describe:

- How you intend to pay attention to yourself. Don't just skim over this process, be intentional on purpose so that you know exactly what not to allow to be mistaken in your life as self-care.

- In this letter, describe what you want your self-care experience to look like and feel like. How well do you want it to make you feel and for how long? Put on paper so that you can remind yourself often how you want to feel after taking care of you.

- Love on you in this letter as if you were falling in love for the first time. Be clear with yourself as to the new routine that you will be putting in place.

Even if you have had a self-care routine in place, go bigger in caring for you. Create a new way that includes mind, body, and spirit. Let the paths of each collide to begin the process of cultivating a new Self-Care routine. Love You! And truly know what self-care is not! Furthermore, doing this you will know that you're on the road to becoming your best self. Journal your emotions! Celebrate you this week.

Week 33

"My Peace is not for sale!"

PEACE

Is a feeling of being safe or protected; a state of tranquility or quiet; a state of security and order. Peace is the freedom of disturbing thoughts or emotions, harmony in personal relationships and the ability to quiet the mind. Peace is the absence of mental stress or anxiety and the absence of worry.

In this state, the mind is quiet, and you experience a sense of happiness and freedom. Often times, we accept things because it has become normal behavior in the course of the relationship. In either case, what you allow to alter your state of being or disturb your peace can begin to put your life in stressful situations. Pay attention to how that makes you feel. If you're comfortable with the interactions you are having with others, great! If not, then spend some time becoming aware of this feeling. Don't overlook it because you think this exercise is not important to you at this stage in your life. Any feelings that allow yourself to push the pause button on, will only keep you stuck in the same types of relationships exhibiting the same types of behavior. Ask yourself:

- Who do I have in my life or circle right now that disturbs my peace of mind when they are around?

....

....

- Who am I constantly engaged in negative conversations with?

....

....

- Who am I holding grudges with or make me uncomfortable to be around?

....

....

Remember own 'Your' power! No one else can own it unless you permit them. Right now, this work may not seem important to you, but trust me, in time you will see why it is.

Week 34

"When your peace of mind is disturbed,
your soul cannot rest."

The Benefits of Peace

Inner Peace (or peace of mind) is a colloquialism that refers to a state of being mentally or spiritually at peace, with enough knowledge and understanding to keep oneself strong in the face of discord or stress. Being "at peace" is considered by many to be healthy and the opposite of being stressed or anxious." Making the mind quiet and calm prevents anxiety, worries, stress, and fears, and awakens inner strength and confidence. Peace of mind is an internal condition and is independent of external conditions and circumstance. When you gain this skill, which by the way can be learned, you remain calm and in control of yourself and your mind, even in the midst of problems and difficult situations. Now that the benefits of peace have been identified:

- Describe what your peace looks like. Fully describe what your peace looks like to you.

....
....

- How are you using your peace to best benefit you?

....
....

- What practices do you have in place for protecting your peace?

....
....

- This week, take daily time to identify what being in your state of peace allowed you to gain.

....
....

- Describe the feelings that you became aware of.

....
....

- What was the gain this week resulting in your peace?

....
....

Find some inner peace this week and center your zone.

Week 35

"Peace doesn't mean to be in a space where there is no movement; it means to be still so that your heart speaks louder than the outside world."

How to Maintain Your Inner Peace

What is inner peace? What I know for sure is that inner peace is something that we all should long for. Inner Peace is a state of being. It's not a place that we go to or a thing we do but something that is deep within us. It is our natural state of being we just have to learn how to let it get through to the surface. Inner Peace isn't something that you must go looking for as it's always there. Finding 'Inner Peace' is about learning to heal those things that prevent us from experiencing our natural state of peace. Since being in a state of inner peace requires us to **know who we are.** Here are some questions that I want you to pay close attention to while journaling this week:

- Can you consciously find a way to worry less and smile more this week?

....

....

- Can you be open, less critical and less judgmental to others?

....

....

- Can you find a way to be more content and appreciative of all the good things in your life?

....

....

- **Can you be more aware to not allow drama and conflict into your life?**

....

....

- Can you let go of the need to worry about your past?

....

....

- Can you find more quiet time without distractions?

....

....

- Can you learn to get still, be quiet and listen to your soul speak to you? Just be in the moment to recognize the beauty that makes you who you are?

....

....

In life "Stuff" still happens, i.e., beliefs, fears, regrets, doubts, anxieties, judgments, anger, and resentment, to name a few. Our inner peace becomes clouded if we allow it, You need to get to a place in your life where you forget 'stuff' exists. Take each day this week to reflect on the above, to be really clear about what your inner peace means to you. Remember to be transparent when it comes to what you are dealing with for peace. Doing the necessary work will allow you to take full responsibility of the power you possess, while, on your journey toward 'Being Your Best'.

Week 36

"The sacredness of my being is dependent on my ability to protect my peace."

Protect Your Peace

Now that you have spent the last few weeks understanding why your peace is so important *is your peace for sale?* Have you allowed any moment of your peace to be taken from you? Pay close attention to the peace killers, and whether or not you're allowing yourself to become a victim. Whether at home, at work, or school, we encounter people who carry with them a variety of "vibes". These people or things, that we have interactions with, are the conduits of their own unique set of vibes which are like a snake sneaking up on you, wrapping its self around you and tightening its grip on you. When their vibe grips you in that manner, you're left to feel defenseless. Sometimes, it manifests itself in feeling overwhelmed and powered by anger, sadness, anxiety or a combination of them all.

Often we encounter these peace killers that leave us feeling depleted, but we hesitate to confront the situation directly. You figure if you don't think about it, it won't bother you as much, but in hind sight, it lays there festering, until the next situation occurs. Confronting toxic peace killers or situations, can be done in many ways. Of course, this is going to depend on your level of confrontation, as well as your reflections on possible outcomes. The key factor here is to remember that you are *inherently worthy of a peaceful lifestyle* and your overall wellness is a priority. The first thing you must always remember is: *Decide* to *protect* your peace!

While it takes some repeated efforts to remember the requirements for balance in all the areas of your life, I know for sure that if my peace is disturbed, then my world is in chaos.

- Journal daily this week if your peace has been interrupted. How it was interrupted and what you did to restore order.

....

- Create a list of ways of staying in control of your peace.

....

- Create your Peace Mantra. I have adopted the saying "My Peace Is Not For Sale!

....
....

Try it out…trust me, it works!

Week 37

"Self-Love is the greatest love of all,"

Learning to Love You

Here is a question, I know it's probably going to sound dumb, but here goes… *Do You Know If You Love Yourself?* Yeah, go ahead and ask yourself again. Here is an even better question to ask yourself, *How Do I Know If I Love Me?* Let me tell you how simple this process is, if you're not *Telling Yourself* how much you *Love Yourself,* you're not really in love with YOU! Simple words that you can express to those that you care about, how much do you really care about You!

Let's start something different and very easy for this week. Every morning when you wake up before you even get out of bed, tell yourself, *I Love Me!* Then, when you head into the bathroom to wash your face or brush your teeth, look into the mirror and say, *I Love You!* Then, I want you to repeat this same thing at night before you go to bed.

Once you get into the habit of *Really Loving You,* watch how things change. Sometimes people think of "loving themselves" as a feeling that you have to conjure up. A good way to look at loving yourself is by emphasizing the action. Answer this question with an open heart:

- What can I Do to love myself?

....
....

Over time, you will discover that loving yourself improves everything in your life. Watch how your self-care will become more important to you. Get ready for some real life changes. It's all about the language you use with yourself; we covered that, remember? It's destined to happen. What you tell yourself you become. What a beautiful feeling it is to be *In Love With You*! In your journaling this week, each day, identify a different way that you can be in the moment of loving yourself. Pay attention to the emotions that surface and be transparent in them.

....
....
....
....
....
....

Week 38

"I see love; I feel love, I touch love,
I hear love, I give love, I show love;
I am love…In Action."

Love Yourself In Action

So, how was last week? Were there any connections made? Unless you connect with self, you really cannot say that you know if you love yourself. You can look fabulous on the outside yet feel miserable on the inside. The most important decision of your life, the one that will affect every other decision you make, is the commitment to love and accept yourself. Love directly affects the quality of your relationships, your work, your time, and your future.

We're taught at a very young age that our worth is based on material things or based on fame and fortune. Your inner self will flood you with the beliefs that you're not enough or lack something. The feeling of worthiness requires you to see yourself in self-awareness and love. We may be taught to bury our magnificence, but it is impossible to destroy. Work is needed on your part to own and appreciate who you are to yourself. Remind yourself daily, that you are worthy of love, and who is better to tell you, then you!

- Take this week to get emotionally honest with yourself. Have you been in love with you?

....

....

- Take a minute to look within to remind yourself how grateful you are for being you.

....

....

Train your mind to accept your brilliance and beauty. Love your perfectly imperfect self.

....

....

Pay attention this week to what makes you feel good and what is keeping you from feeling good. Once you realize the importance of 'Loving You' unconditionally, you will not allow others or things to get in the way of you feeling your best. I challenge you to journal each day if you love yourself enough to correct the things that cause your day to be interrupted. Notice 'You' this week.

Week 39

"There is no competition; no one can love me the way I love me. They can only enhance the love I already show myself,"

Love In Confidence

Confidence comes from the 'Love' you feel for yourself inside. Loving you takes on a whole new definition when you allow nothing to keep you from your happiness, your peace, and ability to love yourself. Loving Your Self is not a one-time event, but an ongoing process. We spend our lives looking for the acceptance to be loved by others when the real love we need comes from within. Loving yourself becomes a state of self-sufficient fulfillment. When you love in confidence of who you are, you can:

- Let go of past beliefs that are keeping you stuck on pause about growing in love with you. Let go of the stories that plague you from healing. Those stories no longer serve the person you're becoming.

....

....

- Allow self-forgiveness to happen before you move forward with learning to love you in confidence. The absence of pain, achieved through healing, gives you the right foundation for deep lasting forgiveness.

....

....

Write in your journal daily to release yourself from any hindrances of embracing a more confident you. Happiness, Peace, and Love are all important parts of your self-care.

....
....
....
....
....
....
....
....
....
....
....

Week 40

The most amazing time you can ever have is with you, Celebrate each moment like it's the first time.

Celebrate the Love of You

Celebrate this week by *Loving On You!* Take time to notice the little things that make you smile. Get in touch with the feeling you have when you are happy. Control your mind to allow nothing but positive thoughts enter your space. Take that longer than usual bath this week. Spend time walking through the park. Eat a little extra cake. Whatever may come your way to diminish your happiness, find a way to shift it to a good place. Find the time every day this week to celebrate you, knowing that the small wins are just as important as the big ones.

Journal your discovery on how it feels to fall in love with you and what've you celebrated this week. Describe how this win of the day made you feel. Create an opportunity for the next day to empower you to love the life you're building.

Week 41

"Be fearless in the pursuit of whatever sets your soul on fire!"

Becoming Fearless

What sets your soul on fire when you speak of it? What keeps you awake at night thinking about it? The only way to become fearless about something you're passionate about is just to do it and work just outside of your comfort zone.

- Start listing the things that you've placed on pause. Do not cheat yourself in this process.

....
....

- Get yourself excited about new possibilities of creating new things for you.

....
....

- Don't underestimate your power to do whatever it is you set your mind to. Don't be afraid to ask for help.

....
....

Loving You, Being at Peace, and Being in Control has a way of releasing the pause in many areas of your life. Get to journaling, and by now you should be clear on how detailed you need to be as you're re creating a new life.

....
....
....
....
....
....
....
....
....
....

Week 42

*"When you are busy in the work
of becoming your best, being open
is the key."*

Be Busy Becoming You

When 'Being Your Best', you don't have time to worry about what someone isn't doing. You're too busy in the work of creating, and becoming more successful. Surround yourself with like-minded people who you can team up with to become even more powerful. Filling your mind with your own business helps you to focus on your master plan. Be who you truly are and don't downplay yourself in front of others. Identify your strengths and weakness. They are markers from which all your progress will be measured. Becoming your best will require you to do a few things. Take this week to consider the following:

- Ignore what others think of you.
- Know who you are.
- Make time for you.
- Take steps daily to learn something new.
- Live in the moment. Be present.
- Forgive yourself often for your mistakes.

Go and claim your power, design your destiny, and become your greatest you! Don't forget to allow yourself to be present in the moment of what you may be thinking or feeling this week. See where these things are showing up for you and how they are playing a part in your daily routine. Be honest in your assessment of yourself. It can only help you to release the pause button to your greatness.

Week 43

"The eyes see one thing, and the tongue says another, but the body speaks a language that all can understand."

Check Your Body Language

While you are on your journey toward 'Being Your Best!', pay close attention to how you interact with the people you come in contact with on a daily basis. Your work this week is to analyze how people treat you and how you receive them.

- Pay close attention to the body language that is being exhibited.

....
....

- Determine if your space is being invaded or if there is a happy distance between you. Your body language speaks volumes when it comes to how others define you.

....
....

- Is your body language one that is welcoming or is it withdrawn?

....
....

Journal your interactions this week, pay attention to the body language you're displaying to others. Notice the body language of others toward you when interacting. Describe what you feel from others and the perception that they may have of you. Let the process of becoming your best with understanding what body is saying begin and be open and honest with this process. You will discover many possibilities of body language this week.

....
....
....
....
....
....
....
....

181

Week 44

"Integrity of the soul brings peace to mind. Never compromise who you are and most certainly, never apologize for it."

Live in Integrity

Living in integrity means that you will not allow anyone to make you compromise your standards. Being able to sleep well at night is a beautiful thing. I never allow anyone to make me feel bad about a decision that I made for me. Remember, you're the only one who has to own up to the choices you make for you. *No One Else*. Never should you feel the need to apologize to anyone for being integral for the decision is for you, no one else. When you walk in integrity:

(1) You become more valuable both as a person and as an achiever, (2) people see your importance and value you, (3) you make better choices, (4) you develop positive habits, (5) you keep your agreements, (6) you become a motivator to others. As you are on your journey toward 'being your best', bear in mind some basic principles:

- Embrace the "aha" moments. If you are fortunate enough to experience those moments in life where things come together, when through your actions you seize the day and utilize golden opportunities, you're able to create lasting changes in life and realize goals. Living your life in integrity means that you're living to your potential, as well as, creating and manifesting your destiny. When truly aligned with our life's purpose, it's easy to stay committed to your goals and dreams and feel fulfillment on a daily basis.

....
....

- Being truly aligned is something that takes regular practice.

When you reach the point in your life where all is going according to your plan, if you start to feel a bit uncomfortable, embrace it. The feeling is life's way of letting you know that the discomfort is your destiny calling in distress.

....
....

- Don't forget about paying it forward. When you are living your life 'Being Your Best' in integrity, there is no such thing as something for nothing. You have to understand the power of giving back and helping someone else to reach their destiny.

....
....

Begin to journal this process. Be clear in your integrity and step into your "aha" moment.

Week 45

"Your opinion matters, but so does others. Everyone has the right to own their opinion."

Opinions

Have you ever been in conversation with someone and you zoned out because they just refused to get your point? I most certainly have. What I've come to realize is that, for as much as I feel my opinion matters to me, so does other people. We all have the right to "own" our view. And the understanding of the definition has made my decision easier to allow something not necessarily based on fact or knowledge to aggravate me. Once I begin to go into all of my conversations this way, my level of conversation changed. As much as I may not agree with someone's opinion, I realize that they are entitled to it.

It can be so refreshing not to allow things to bother you that have no direct bearing on you. And most importantly, never make what doesn't have to be an issue become one.

- Can you recall a time (s) where your conversation became a bit unpleasant because your opinion differed from someone else'?

....

....

- Now that you are on your journey toward 'Being Your Best', what would you have done differently to prevent anyone to take you out of character?

....

....

Spend this week implementing how you would put this into practice. Watch how different your conversations become.

....
....
....
....
....
....
....
....

Week 46

"Your legacy is not to leave something "for" people it's to leave something "in" people. Leave them amazed."

How will you be remembered?

When I realized that only I could see life how I wanted to live, it became apparent to me the type of legacy I wanted to leave. No matter if you chose to believe it or not, you're being looked on by others. How you're living now, will determine what others will reflect and remember about you once you are no longer here.

- What memories are you making that will leave them in *Awe*?

....

....

- What will be the greatest part of your legacy for all to remember?

....

....

Reflect this week on how you are showing up in the world. Are you satisfied with your results? It's not too late but hurry, because there's no promise for tomorrow only the faith that we will make it to the next day. Show them that you are leaving a legacy where you will be your best!

....
....
....
....
....
....
....
....
....
....
....
....
....
....

Week 47

"From the sounds of your lips to the sway of your hips, 'Being Your Best' is not a #hashtag, it's a way you begin to move, walk and talk through life!"

"Being Your Best" is all that anyone can ask of you

When you really understand the magnitude of living a life "Being Your Best," no one can ask more of you. What do I mean by this? 'Being Your Best' is not a #hashtag, it's a way of life that encompasses everything you do, say, even the way you think and changes you for good. Being as transparent as you can, take this week to list the areas of your life that you know you need to work on to live a life "Being Your Best." Don't be surprised if you feel your list is long as no one is perfect. What this will do is bring to your conscious the things you have to start working on. Be as transparent as you can as this is your life, and you want the best for you because you love you. Search to see if:

- Are you true to who you really are?

....

....

- Are you as proactive as you can be with your life?

....

....

- Are your creating new possibilities for yourself?

....

....

- Do you still have parts of your life pressed on pause for fear of what you may discover about you?

....

....

- Are you open to growth?

....

....

- Are you living your life's purpose?

....

....

Even if you don't feel as if you have all the answers to the above questions, take this week to pick them apart one by one to discover the possibility that you unfold.

Week 48

"I Am because I tell myself "I Can Be,"
I make no apologies as I go about things,
in my way."

Self Doubt

You have heard me reminding you throughout this journal the importance of making no apologies to anyone for your life. I have been told many times in my life that I wouldn't excel at things. I used to say to myself "Why, because "YOU" say so? Those words would "get my goat," as my Aunt Pat used to say. We tell children whom we love that they can be anything that they set their minds to be, why is it that "We" don't believe that same thing at adulthood? When you doubt yourself, you have already given the doubt the power. Trust in yourself to use what you have inside to create. With the right attitude, you can bring any goal into existence. The choice that one has when doing anything in life is to:

- Believe in yourself, or

- Allow yourself to be sucked into self-pity and feelings of self-doubt.

And, you can do it however you choose, it's that simple. It's often easier to alleviate fears and doubts and to gain clarity if you put your thoughts on paper or your laptop instead of allowing them to run rampant in your mind. Making the list of your pros and cons can help you create a clear plan of action to break the mold of the self-doubt.

Each day this week, I want you to identify an area where you allowed someone to talk you out of something and check to see if that "thing" would benefit you now. If it does, make a plan of action to go for it.

....
....
....
....
....
....
....
....
....

Week 49

"The Journey of a thousand miles begins with one single step."

Walk into the New Journey, loving the New You

If you have stayed the course, you're about to be complete your first year of work on *You*! Without a doubt in my mind, this has been a year of awakening in some areas of your life that you were possibly stuck on pause. This week, spend time reflecting on the areas you've seen growth? List a few of the areas where you can see that you have chosen to release the pause button.

- How clear are you regarding the direction your life is taking you?

....

....

- How content are you at this stage of growth in your life. Are you satisfied with where you are, or do you see yourself doing/wanting more?

....

....

- How open are you with your thoughts and feelings regarding your life's plans? Are you of letting others in that may be able to help you get to the next level in your life?

....

....

- Are you open to trying new things?

....

....

As you learned throughout this journal, change can be a good thing. Spend time reflecting on the changes you've made that have been good for you. Remember to include the areas that benefited you the most. It's important to remind yourself of the shift you've made toward 'Becoming Your Best.' Life should be looking much brighter for you...enjoy the journey!

Week 50

It's through adversity we've learned to endure, we gain the strength to design the life we want to live."

Designing the Life, You Want

Now that you have identified areas of growth, let's not stop there. The time is now to challenge yourself to do new and exciting things you have always wanted to do. Take a look at the past year and see if there is anything you can see yourself doing now that you have released the pause button. Ask yourself:

- Have I identified my real purpose in life and what that looks like for me? Draw out that detailed plan of life for yourself. Set the stage for your new beginning, not allowing anyone to dictate this for you. Be clear an open and ready to take on the responsibility to own your power. Get Busy!

....

....

- While creating this new motion picture, which you're the star, what does your value system look like? What are some ways of being and doing that you won't allow to creep back into your life now that you are on the road to 'Being Your Best'? It is important that you're clear about your values, so you can make the best choices when it matters the most.

....

- Are you doing enough for YOU! Answering this question honestly can have a dramatic effect on you and where you are going in your life. The more you understand your life and how you want it to work, the greater your chances of success will be. The beauty in all of this is you get to create the exact life that you want to live; you will make more effective decisions about your life and the actions you need to take for the success of your decisions.

....

....

The Time Is Now! What are you waiting for? Get Busy! Level Up!

....

....

Week 51

"The mind is like a parachute, remember, it doesn't work unless it's opened."

Have An Open Mind

It's been an interesting year, and you have spent some quality time working on You. What would you say was the one thing you're most happy that you took the time to work on to become the best you? Were you open for the change? Achieving personal goals requires a great deal of personal growth and change. However, once reached, the element of this shift and what it took to get there is often forgotten. The lapse in memory allows you to fall back into old habits and ways of being. Resistance to change can be one of the biggest factors in failing to achieve longevity in maintaining the goals you previously met. It's a form of self-sabotage! Before you forget how you got to become this new you, it is important to do this one thing:

- Write yourself a letter identifying the area of change you have made and what roads it took to get you there. Don't leave out one thing, as this letter will become your reminder as to why it's important to maintain your integrity in staying the course for change.
  Remind yourself in this letter how different your life has become because of this change, but more importantly, what it is that you like about your life, since your change, and the effect that it has had on others. Have they noticed? Have you seen any changes in them? This letter will be your reminder as to why you need to stay the course when times may seem a little rough, and you feel your old self, start to surface.

Embrace this part of your journey; it will be the best thing you could have done for you.

....
....
....
....
....
....
....
....
....

Week 52

"To give freely of yourself with no hidden agenda will bring forth riches that cannot be measured by money or things!"

DECLARATION

I declare today that I will continue to work on me. I will not take my self-care for granted and will continue the healing process in the area I still struggle with. I know that I am still a work in progress but will continue to do everything that I can to work towards, BEING MY BEST!

Take this last week to reflect on the past year. Identify the area that you may need to continue to work on. Don't forget to celebrate your wins of the previous year.

Conclusion

In these past 52 weeks, you've explored all of the above topics and then some. This process hopefully began to get you started on the road to self-care discovery, allowing you the chance to release the pause on what has kept you stuck.

Over the next week, go over your journal to see where you need to pay more attention. Remember we are all a continuing work in progress. I'm humbled that you took the time to do this work. It's only the beginning of discovering the "New You"! Welcome to the self-discovery process of "BEING YOUR BEST. "

It's not how you start the process on your road to becoming your best; it's how you finish.

CPSIA information can be obtained
at www.ICGtesting.com
Printed in the USA
FSOW02n1049161117
41229FS

9 780999 386002